TALLINN TRAVEL GUIDE 2024

PRACTICAL TIPS ON HISTORY, CULTURE AND ADVENTURE

ANGELA RENNER

Copyright © 2024 Angela Renner

All rights reserved.

No part of this book may be reproduced in any form without written permission from the author, except for brief quotations in a review or scholarly work. This includes electronic, mechanical, photocopying, recording, or any other information retrieval system.

Table of Contents

Chapter One
Introduction to Tallinn
        Historical Background
        Modern Tallinn
        Why Visit Tallinn in 2024

Chapter Two
Updated 2024 Information
        Overcoming Language Barriers
        Managing Travel Delays and Disruptions
        Tips for a Smooth Transition
        Managing Transportation Challenges
        What to Do If You Misplaced Your Belongings
        Healthcare and Safety
        Currency Management
        Cultural Etiquette
        Solutions to Challenges of Solo Travelers
        Sim Card and Internet Issues
        Frequently Asked Questions

Chapter Three
Practical Travel Tips
        Travel Tips for Introverts
        Travel Backpacks
        Restaurants / What to Eat
        Gastronomic Delights
        Gifts to Buy

    What to Do On Long Flights
    What to Pack
    Visa and Entry Requirements
    Weather and Best Time to Go
    Souvenir and Shopping
    Navigation and Map
    Popular Markets
    Suggested Itinerary
    Useful Language Phrases
Chapter Four
Must-See Attractions
    Tallinn Old Town
    Kadriorg Palace and Park
    Seaplane Harbour
    Alexander Nevsky Cathedral
    Telliskivi Creative City
Chapter Five
Top Cities Near Tallinn
    Helsinki, Finland
    Riga, Latvia
    St. Petersburg, Russia
    Stockholm, Sweden
    Vilnius, Lithuania
    Turku, Finland
    Tartu, Estonia
    Pärnu, Estonia
    Kaunas, Lithuania
    Narva, Estonia
Chapter Six

The Top Hidden Gems
- Kalamaja District
- Estonian Maritime Museum
- St. Bridget's Convent Ruins
- Nõmme Market
- Kumu Art Museum

Chapter Seven

Accommodation Options
- Hotel and Resort
- Low Budget Accommodations
- Unique Accommodation
- Booking Tip and Recommendations

Chapter Eight

Transportation System and Cautions
- Public Transportation Overview
- Renting A Vehicle
- Precautions for Travelers

Chapter Nine

Top Beaches
- Pirita Beach
- Stroomi Beach
- Kakumäe Beach
- Pikakari Beach
- Rohuneeme Beach

Chapter Ten

Cultural Experiences
- Local Festivities and Events
- Historic and Cultural Tours
- Special Experiences for Travelers

Chapter Eleven
Useful Tips for Tourists and Travelers
- Currency and Payment
- Language
- Public Transport
- Walk Tours
- Weather Considerations
- Internet Connectivity
- Safety
- Open Hours
- Local Cuisine
- Tap Water
- Sunset on Toompea Hill
- Day Trips
- Estonian Saunas
- Local Event Calendar
- Photo Etiquette
- Emergency Service
- Tipping Etiquette
- Cultural Sensitivity
- Local Markets
- Pack Accordingly

Chapter Twelve
Other Resources
- Travel Apps for Exploring Tallinn
- Essential Websites for Tallinn Visitors
- Local Services and Contacts
- Cultural and Historical Resources
- Social Media and Online Communities

- Educational and Entertainment Resources
- Sustainable Travel Resources
- Bus Lines in Tallinn
- Where to Find Bus Lines
- Popular Bus Lines and Destinations
- Warnings and Tips for Travelers

Conclusion

Chapter One

Introduction to Tallinn

Tallinn, Estonia's charming city, entices visitors with its rich history, vibrant culture, and breathtaking scenery. Tallinn, located on the Baltic Sea's northern coast, is a city that combines medieval elegance and modern refinement. Tallinn, Estonia's largest city and a major participant in the Baltic area, provides a distinct blend of heritage and innovation, making it a must-see destination for tourists looking for a genuine European experience.

Tallinn's core is the UNESCO-listed Old Town, a surprisingly well-preserved medieval city that transports tourists back in time. Cobblestone streets wind between historic buildings, revealing a great component of architectural styles that reflect the city's unique history. From the famous Tallinn Town Hall to the magnificent Alexander Nevsky Cathedral, the city's icons tell stories of perseverance and cultural progress.

Beyond its historic core, Tallinn has a vibrant metropolitan landscape. Modern buildings lie side by side with centuries-old structures, creating an intriguing contrast. The city is a technological and innovation hotspot, receiving the nickname "e-Estonia" for its excellent digital infrastructure.

Tallinn's allure extends to the gorgeous surroundings. The city is surrounded by lush greenery, and parks and gardens provide peaceful getaways. The Baltic Sea provides breathtaking views and a fresh maritime environment. Tallinn promises a voyage through time as well as a celebration of Estonia's perseverance and growth, whether you meander through the charming streets of the Old Town or explore the city's modern aspects.

Historical Background

Tallinn's history dates back to the early Middle Ages, when German merchants established it as a trading hub in the 13th century. Over the ages, the city has become a cultural melting pot, affected by German, Danish, Russian, and Swedish control. Its advantageous placement along important trade routes aided its economic growth and cultural variety.

The Hanseatic League, a prominent medieval commercial association, was instrumental in creating Tallinn's fortunes. The city thrived as a league member, which added to its architectural magnificence and economic prominence. Tallinn, on the other hand, has seen times of conflict and conquest, as well as foreign occupations.

In the twentieth century, Estonia endured the challenges of two World Wars and subsequent Soviet occupation. Tallinn became a key area of resistance during the Singing Revolution, a nonviolent movement that helped Estonia achieve independence in 1991. This stormy history is woven throughout the city's streets, lending layers of meaning to its landmarks.

Tallinn stands today as a tribute to its people's tenacity and dedication to preserving their cultural heritage. Tallinn's intriguing combination of medieval elegance and modern progress draws visitors to study its rich past.

Modern Tallinn

Modern Tallinn blends harmoniously with its historical roots, resulting in a dynamic cityscape that reflects Estonia's transformation into a technological powerhouse. Tallinn is no longer a city locked in time by 2024, but rather a thriving metropolis that embraces innovation while keeping its cultural character.

Tallinn's contemporary identity is best reflected in its technological developments. The city has established itself as a digital pioneer, with a strong startup environment and a commitment to e-governance. Tallinn's innovative approach is exemplified by the notion of e-residency, which allows people from all over the world to establish a digital presence in Estonia. The city's dedication to technology is evident, with free public Wi-Fi, digital public services, and smart urban planning, making it a sanctuary for IT fans.

In addition to its technological strength, modern Tallinn has a vibrant arts and entertainment scene. The city is a creative hotspot, with various art galleries, theaters, and cultural festivals. Contemporary Estonian artists add to the city's cultural diversity by combining historic inspirations with current viewpoints. Tallinn's dedication to cultural vibrancy is demonstrated by its selection as a European Capital of Culture in 2011.

Tallinn's gastronomic environment reflects its modernity, with a varied selection of restaurants serving both traditional Estonian food and cosmopolitan influences. Food markets and culinary festivals provide both locals and visitors a taste of the city's culinary innovations. Tallinn's eating experience is pleasurable and diversified, thanks to a blend of old-world elegance and new culinary trends.

Why Visit Tallinn in 2024

Tallinn welcomes visitors in 2024 with a persuasive list of reasons to explore its lovely streets and embrace its distinct atmosphere. Tallinn, with its rich history and current attractiveness, stands out as a place that offers an immersive and gratifying experience.

One of the main reasons to visit Tallinn in 2024 is its UNESCO World Heritage Site classification. The Old Town's well-preserved medieval architecture and cobblestone streets transport visitors back in time. Tallinn's dedication to conserving its historical legacy guarantees that every nook tells a narrative, offering an unmatched environment for history buffs.

Tallinn is a popular destination for cultural events and festivals, in addition to its historical significance. The city's dynamic cultural scene, which includes exhibitions and performances, provides an exciting setting for visitors looking to engage with current Estonian culture. Travelers in 2024 can immerse themselves in the city's creative spirit, explore local artists' abilities, and see the blend of tradition and innovation.

Tallinn's status as a technologically advanced and innovative city is another enticing reason to visit. Tallinn, the birthplace of Skype and a pioneer in e-governance, represents the future of digital living. Exploring the city's technical landscape reveals Estonia's dedication to progress and offers a unique viewpoint on the junction of tradition and contemporary.

Tallinn remains a naturalist's paradise in 2024. The city is surrounded by beautiful scenery, which provides chances for outdoor activities such as hiking, cycling, and exploring the adjacent islands. The Baltic Sea serves as a refreshing backdrop for relaxation and maritime excursions, making Tallinn a great location for anyone seeking a balance of urban exploration and natural beauty.

Tallinn's warm atmosphere, cultural diversity, and forward-thinking mindset make it a top choice for travelers in 2024. Tallinn welcomes visitors who are intrigued by its historical charm, keen to experience its modern inventions, or looking for a combination of the two.

Chapter Two

Updated 2024 Information

Staying up to date on the most recent developments and important details is critical for a successful and easy trip to Tallinn in 2024. This area provides you with the most up-to-date and relevant information to ensure that your trip plans are in line with the current landscape. This updated information covers everything from visa procedures to local legislation and events, ensuring that visitors have an enriching and hassle-free experience in Tallinn.

Check for any current travel advisories, entrance procedures, and health guidelines. Stay informed on local events, festivals, and exhibitions to make the most of your visit. Use online tools, government tourism websites, and local news to keep up with any changes that may affect your travel plans.

Overcoming Language Barriers

While Tallinn is a hospitable city, overcoming potential language obstacles might improve your visit experience. The official language is Estonian, however many inhabitants, particularly in cities, are fluent in English. Learning a few basic Estonian phrases can be a fun way to engage with the locals and demonstrate cultural respect.

To overcome language barriers, try using translation apps or carrying a pocket-sized phrasebook. These technologies can aid with basic communication, such as navigating menus, asking for directions, and engaging in casual discussions. Furthermore, being sensitive to nonverbal communication, such as gestures and expressions, can help to bridge language barriers and promote productive interactions.

In tourist-friendly places, signage and information are frequently available in English. However, deviating from the usual path may necessitate a bit more linguistic flexibility. Embracing the local language, even in tiny doses, can improve your practical experience while also endearing you to the local population.

Managing Travel Delays and Disruptions

Travel arrangements are sometimes susceptible to unforeseen delays and disruptions. Understanding how to manage these situations can make a big difference in the overall success of your vacation. Stay up to date on flight delays and cancellations by checking airline notifications and announcements. Have a backup plan in place, such as contact information for local hotels or alternate transit options.

Consider getting travel insurance to reduce the financial risks connected with unexpected disruptions. Many plans cover trip cancellations, delays, and emergency medical costs. Familiarize yourself with your insurance's terms and conditions to ensure it matches your individual requirements.

Maintain a calm and adaptable attitude in the event of a travel inconvenience. Airport and transit officials are there to help, and civility can go a long way toward resolving concerns. Use communication channels like the airline's customer service hotline or social media to stay up to date on the newest news.

By proactively preparing for language obstacles and anticipated travel disruptions, you empower yourself to easily handle unexpected challenges, enabling you to focus on enjoying Tallinn's dynamic offerings.

Tips for a Smooth Transition

Jet lag can be a difficult foe for anyone traveling time zones to reach Tallinn. To ensure a smooth adjustment and make the most of your time in the city, use smart jet lag solutions. Begin changing your sleep routine a few days before departure to coincide with Tallinn's local time. Maintain hydration throughout the travel, avoid excessive coffee and alcohol consumption, and expose yourself to natural light upon landing. These routines help reset your internal clock, reducing the effects of jet lag and allowing you to dive into Tallinn's offerings with vigor and excitement.

Creating a pleasant sleeping environment upon arrival is critical. To promote healthy sleep, use blackout curtains, keep the room temperature temperate, and stick to a nighttime routine.

Light physical activity, such as taking a leisurely stroll, can also assist balance your circadian cycle. Prioritizing rest and gradual acclimatization will prepare you to enjoy Tallinn's attractions from the time you arrive.

Managing Transportation Challenges

Efficient transportation is essential for a successful visit, and knowing how to manage potential obstacles ensures a more enjoyable travel experience in Tallinn. Familiarize yourself with the city's public transit, which includes buses, trams, and trolleys. Consider getting a transit card for more convenience and savings.

If you intend to rent a vehicle, be aware of local traffic and parking requirements. Tallinn's tiny city center is best explored on foot, although for greater distances or day trips, dependable transit options exist. Taxis, ride-sharing applications, and bike rentals provide flexible transportation options.

Keep track of anticipated traffic disruptions by checking local news or transportation authority announcements. In the event of an unexpected issue, have backup plans and contact information for alternate transportation options. Planning ahead of time and keeping flexible can allow you to easily explore Tallinn, ensuring that you arrive at your intended destinations on time and enjoy the city's unique experiences.

What to Do If You Misplaced Your Belongings

While Tallinn is generally a safe destination, visitors should be prepared for the unexpected, such as lost or stolen possessions. Use anti-theft items like money belts to protect your possessions, and keep vital documents in a travel pouch. Make photocopies of crucial documents, including your passport, and keep them separate from the originals.

In the case that your belongings are lost or stolen, notify local police and your lodging provider right once. Keep a list of key phone numbers, such as your embassy or consulate, and contact your bank to report any stolen cards.

Travel insurance is vital for reducing the cost impact of lost or stolen belongings. Familiarize yourself with your insurance coverage, including how to file a claim. Many insurance companies provide coverage for lost baggage, personal property, and theft-related expenditures.

Remaining cautious and proactive in protecting your things, combined with a contingency plan for the worst-case scenario, can help you manage any problems smoothly, allowing you to concentrate on the wonderful experiences in Tallinn.

Healthcare and Safety

When visiting a new place like Tallinn, it's critical to prioritize your health and safety. Before your journey, make sure you are up to date on normal immunizations and look into any unique health concerns for Estonia. Carry a basic first-aid kit that includes pills, bandages, and any prescription drugs you may need.

It is recommended to obtain travel insurance that includes medical emergencies and evacuation. Familiarize yourself with the locations of medical services in Tallinn, such as hospitals and pharmacies, and save emergency contact information in your phone. To avoid potential gastrointestinal troubles, consume local water and food with caution, and maintain excellent hygiene to limit the transmission of infections.

In the event of a medical emergency, seek immediate aid and notify your embassy or consulate. Following basic health and safety precautions can help you have a relaxing and pleasurable time in Tallinn.

Currency Management

Currency exchange is an important part of managing funds during your trip to Tallinn. Estonia's national currency is the Euro (EUR), which is widely accepted across the country. Research current exchange rates and be aware of any potential currency conversion expenses.

Optimize your financial planning by withdrawing cash from Tallinn's numerous ATMs. Major credit cards are accepted at most locations, but it's a good idea to have some cash for smaller transactions and places that don't accept cards.

Be wary of currency exchange frauds and only use legitimate exchange services, such as banks or authorized currency exchange offices. To avoid card troubles, keep track of your expenses, review your account records on a regular basis, and notify your bank of your travel dates.

Staying knowledgeable about currency exchange processes and taking a multifaceted approach to managing your finances can ensure a pleasant and secure financial experience while visiting Tallinn.

Cultural Etiquette

Respecting local customs and cultural norms is vital for an enjoyable and culturally stimulating stay in Tallinn. Estonia has a distinct cultural character, and being aware of proper etiquette will improve your relationships with locals.

Greet individuals with a pleasant "Tere!" (Hello!) and be cordial in all encounters. Estonians appreciate personal space and hence keep a comfortable distance during interactions. When welcomed to someone's home, bring a small gift like flowers to show your appreciation.

Understanding the significance of cultural events and holidays, such as Midsummer's Day or Independence Day, enables you to connect with your community. Avoid delicate questions about Estonia's history and geopolitical status unless the conversation organically moves in that direction.

Dress modestly when visiting holy locations, and always take off your shoes before entering someone's home. Embracing these cultural nuances shows respect for Tallinn's traditions and promotes positive relationships with the community. By managing cultural etiquette with sensitivity, you may ensure that your stay in Tallinn is not only enjoyable but also culturally enriching.

Solutions to Challenges of Solo Travelers

A single trip to Tallinn provides a unique and enriching experience, but it also has its own set of problems. To get the most out of your solo vacation, you must handle these problems ahead of time.

One major fear among solitary travelers is safety. Learn about the local emergency services and share your itinerary with someone you trust. Choose hotels in well-traveled regions and use caution when exploring unknown districts, particularly after dark. Joining group excursions or activities is a great way to meet other travelers and form a sense of community.

Loneliness is another issue that solitary travelers may confront. Participate in social activities, such as guided tours or local gatherings, to meet like-minded people. Use social media platforms and travel forums to connect with other lone travelers in Tallinn, developing potential friendships.

Language barriers may be more noticeable for single travelers. Learn some basic Estonian language, bring a translation software, and be open to nonverbal communication. This effort not only helps with navigation, but also promotes beneficial connections with locals.

Solo travelers should keep their itinerary flexible. Unexpected possibilities may happen, and having the flexibility to change your plans makes for a more spontaneous and enjoyable experience. Solo travel problems can be addressed with careful planning, an optimistic attitude, and a willingness to face the unexpected, resulting in a very personal and rewarding voyage.

Sim Card and Internet Issues

In an age when keeping connected is critical, dealing with internet connectivity issues while traveling can be irritating. In Tallinn, however, dealing with this difficulty is very simple.

To ensure ongoing connectivity, consider acquiring a local SIM card when you arrive. Estonia has good mobile network coverage, and purchasing a local SIM card allows you to enjoy reasonable data plans for internet access. Major public venues, motels, and cafes also have free Wi-Fi, giving visitors more ways to remain connected.

A virtual private network (VPN) is recommended for secure browsing, particularly while utilizing public Wi-Fi. This provides an additional degree of safety for your critical information.

In the event of an internet outage, have offline maps and crucial information downloaded ahead. This ensures that you can navigate the city and obtain critical information even without an active internet connection.

By tackling internet connectivity issues with these options, you'll be able to stay connected, share your experiences, and access critical information during your stay in Tallinn, enhancing your vacation experience in this interesting city.

Frequently Asked Questions

Solo travel, particularly to a new destination like Tallinn, frequently brings a slew of questions for eager adventurers. To ensure you start your journey well-informed, here are 20 frequently asked questions and detailed answers:

Q: Is Tallinn safe for single travelers?

A: Yes, Tallinn is typically regarded as safe for single tourists. If you take the usual measures, you should find yourself in a friendly and safe environment.

Q: What is the local currency in Tallinn?

A: The official currency is the Euro (EUR).
Q. Do I need a visa to visit Tallinn?

A: Estonia is part of the Schengen Area, and depending on your nationality, you may or may not need a visa for short stays. Check the criteria prior to your trip.

Q. Is English widely spoken in Tallinn?

A: Yes, English is commonly spoken, particularly in tourist destinations.

Q: How do I use public transit in Tallinn?

A: Tallinn's public transit system is efficient and includes buses, trams, and trolleys. Consider getting a transit card for convenience.

Q. When is the ideal time to visit Tallinn?

A: Summer (June to August) has beautiful weather and longer days, making it an excellent season to visit Tallinn.

Q: How can I deal with jet lag while traveling to Tallinn?

A: Change your sleep routine before leaving, stay hydrated, and expose yourself to natural light upon arrival.

Q: Are there any health issues in Tallinn?

A: Tallinn is typically considered safe in terms of health. Ensure that routine vaccines are up to date, and follow normal precautions.

Q. Can I drink tap water in Tallinn?
A: The tap water in Tallinn is safe to drink.

Q: What must-see sights in Tallinn?

Tallinn's Old Town, Alexander Nevsky Cathedral, and Toompea Castle are among the must-see sites.

Q: How should I handle currency exchange?

A: Use trustworthy foreign exchange services, take out cash from ATMs, and be wary of any surcharges.

Q: What should I do if my belongings are lost?

A: Notify local authorities as well as your lodging provider about the event. If required, contact your embassy and consider purchasing travel insurance.

Q: Are there any local SIM cards accessible for internet access?

A: Yes, local SIM cards are widely available, offering reasonable data plans for internet access.

Q: What are the best ways to stay connected in Tallinn?

Aside from cell data, numerous public venues, motels, and cafes provide free Wi-Fi.

Q: How can I interact with the local culture respectfully?

A: Learn a few basic Estonian phrases, respect personal space, and follow local norms, such as removing shoes before entering someone's home.

Q: Can I use a credit card in Tallinn?
A: Major credit cards are commonly accepted.

Q: What is the tipping culture in Tallinn?

A: Tipping is appreciated, but not required. Round up the price or leave a 5-10% tip if the service is outstanding.

Q: What cultural events or festivals should I attend?

A: Check the local calendar for events like Tallinn Music Week and Christmas Markets.

Q: How can I overcome potential language barriers?

A: Learn simple Estonian phrases, use translation apps, and practice nonverbal communication.

Q: Can you rent a bike in Tallinn?

A: Bike rentals are available, providing an environmentally beneficial and convenient way to explore the city.

These commonly asked questions and answers are intended to address common concerns, ensuring that your solo trip to Tallinn is seamless, informative, and memorable.

Chapter Three

Practical Travel Tips

Travel Tips for Introverts

Introverts can easily traverse the dynamic city of Tallinn by employing careful techniques that are tailored to their tastes. Begin by selecting accommodations that provide quiet locations to unwind and refresh. Consider visiting the city during off-peak hours to avoid crowds.

Solo activities, such as self-guided excursions or tranquil walks through parks, allow introverts to experience Tallinn's beauty at their own speed. Use technology to plan and navigate, reducing the need for frequent social engagement.

Enjoy Tallinn's gastronomic delights in a more private environment by dining at neighborhood cafés and quieter areas of restaurants. Finally, take breaks between activities to relax and reflect, ensuring a fulfilling and delightful time in the city.

Travel Backpacks

Choosing the correct travel backpack is essential for a comfortable and orderly trip around Tallinn. Consider size, durability, and features that meet your individual demands. Look for backpacks with various sections, which allow for efficient arrangement of items.

Choose a size that fits your basics without being unduly cumbersome. Make sure the backpack is built of strong materials and can withstand various weather conditions. Padded straps and back support provide extra comfort during extended treks through Tallinn's lovely districts.

Brands like Osprey, Patagonia, and North Face provide a variety of travel bag sizes and features. Research and read reviews to select a backpack that fits your travel style and provides both usefulness and comfort as you explore Tallinn.

Restaurants / What to Eat

Tallinn's culinary scene is diversified and wonderful, with a variety of traditional and international cuisine to suit all tastes. Start your gastronomic journey by eating local Estonian specialties like sült (jellied beef), hõõgvein (mulled wine), and pirukad (savory pastries).

Explore the heart of Tallinn's Old Town to find delightful restaurants serving Estonian cuisine. Rataskaevu 16, for example, is well-known for its modern spin on traditional foods, offering a great culinary experience.

Tallinn has a diverse range of international cuisine options. Telliskivi Creative City is a popular destination for stylish cafes and various restaurants. F-hoone, located in Telliskivi, is renowned for its industrial-chic ambiance and multinational food.

Discover the Baltic and Scandinavian influences in Tallinn's cuisine by sampling fresh fish and substantial Nordic-inspired meals. Local markets, such as Balti Jaama Turg, highlight the city's gastronomic diversity by selling anything from street cuisine to artisanal delights.

Remember to accompany your meals with local beverages such as Vana Tallinn liqueur or craft beers from Estonian producers. Tallinn's diverse dining alternatives make each meal a wonderful voyage through the city's rich culinary past and contemporary gastronomic scene.

Gastronomic Delights

Tallinn's gastronomy scene is a foodie's paradise. Enjoy the rich and diverse flavors that define Estonian cuisine while exploring the city's culinary scene. Begin your culinary journey with the renowned Sült, a jellied meat, and Hõõgvein, an aromatic mulled wine.

Explore local markets like Balti Jaama Turg, where you may try regional specialties and handcrafted products. Try Pirukad, delicious pastries stuffed with meat, cabbage, or cheese, and enjoy the delightful combination of Baltic and Nordic influences.

Rataskaevu 16, a renowned restaurant in Tallinn's Old Town, serves innovative versions of traditional Estonian meals. F-hoone in Telliskivi Creative City serves an eclectic menu in a stylish setting, including a wonderful blend of Estonian and international flavors.

For a sweet finish, try traditional delicacies like Kringel, a cinnamon and nut pastry, or Vahukommi Kohvik, a café famous for its delicious cakes and pastries. Tallinn's gourmet delights promise a culinary trip that reflects both the city's rich cultural history and modern culinary inventiveness.

Gifts to Buy

Selecting thoughtful gifts for friends is an essential part of any travel experience, and Tallinn offers a variety of unique and locally-inspired options. Consider bringing back a bottle of Vana Tallinn, a traditional Estonian liqueur, as a flavorful and distinctive gift.

Estonian handicrafts, such as knitwear or traditional wooden items, showcase the country's rich cultural heritage. Look for handmade ceramics, textiles, or jewelry in local markets or boutique shops to share a piece of Tallinn's artisanal craftsmanship.

For those with a sweet tooth, Estonian chocolate and marzipan are popular choices. Visit the famous Kalev Chocolate Shop to find a selection of sweet treats that reflect Tallinn's confectionery traditions.

Tallinn's vibrant arts scene offers unique souvenirs, such as locally crafted artwork or prints inspired by the city's architecture and landscapes. Explore the galleries in the Old Town or the creative spaces in Telliskivi to discover one-of-a-kind pieces that make for memorable gifts.

Remember, the most cherished gifts often carry a personal touch, so consider items that resonate with your friends' interests and preferences. Whether it's culinary delights, traditional crafts, or artistic treasures, Tallinn provides a plethora of options to find the perfect gifts for your loved ones.

What to Do On Long Flights

Long rides or flights to Tallinn provide an opportunity for relaxation, entertainment, and preparation for the adventures ahead. Pack a good book, magazine, or e-reader to immerse yourself in literature and pass the time during the journey.

Create a personalized travel playlist featuring your favorite tunes or explore Estonian music to set the mood for your Tallinn experience. Podcasts and audiobooks offer informative and entertaining content, making the journey both enjoyable and educational.

Ensure your devices are fully charged and carry a power bank to stay connected and entertained. Download offline maps and travel apps to navigate Tallinn seamlessly, even without an internet connection.

Take advantage of in-flight or in-car Wi-Fi to plan your itinerary, research local attractions, and make reservations. Organize your travel documents, ensuring you have easy access to passports, tickets, and accommodation details.

Hydrate regularly and pack snacks to stay nourished during the journey. Incorporate stretches and simple exercises to prevent stiffness and promote circulation.

By curating a mix of entertainment, planning, and self-care, long rides or flights become an integral part of your Tallinn adventure, setting the stage for a smooth and enjoyable exploration of the captivating Estonian capital.

What to Pack

Packing strategically for your journey to Tallinn ensures you are well-prepared for the diverse experiences the city offers. Begin with essentials such as comfortable walking shoes for exploring Tallinn's charming cobblestone streets. Given Estonia's varying weather, pack layers to adapt to temperature changes.

Include a travel adapter to charge your devices, as Estonia uses the European standard Type F outlets. A portable power bank ensures your devices stay charged during your explorations.

Tallinn experiences both sunny days and occasional rain, so packing a compact umbrella and a waterproof jacket is advisable. A daypack is useful for carrying essentials as you wander through the city.

For cultural and historical explorations, consider a guidebook or map to navigate

Tallinn's landmarks. A reusable water bottle helps you stay hydrated during your walks, and a camera captures the picturesque beauty of the city.

Lastly, pack any specific medications, toiletries, and travel-sized laundry detergent for convenience during your stay.

Visa and Entry Requirements

For travelers to Tallinn, understanding visa and entry requirements is crucial. Estonia is part of the Schengen Area, allowing citizens of many countries to enter visa-free for short stays. However, it's essential to check specific requirements based on your nationality.

Ensure your passport is valid for at least six months beyond your intended departure date. Confirm if you need a visa and apply well in advance, considering processing times. Check the official website of the Estonian government or the embassy in your country for the latest information on visa requirements.

Have supporting documents ready, including proof of accommodation, travel insurance, and a return ticket. Keep a copy of these documents both digitally and in print for easy access.

Remember that entry requirements may vary, so always verify the latest information before your trip. Failure to comply with visa and entry regulations could result in delays or denied entry.

Weather and Best Time to Go

Understanding Tallinn's weather patterns helps in planning an enjoyable and comfortable visit. The best time to explore Tallinn is during the summer months from June to August when the weather is mild and days are long. This is peak tourist season, offering a bustling atmosphere and numerous outdoor events.

Spring (April to May) and early autumn (September to October) also provide pleasant weather, with fewer crowds. During these seasons, you can experience the beauty of blooming flowers in spring or enjoy the changing colors of autumn.

Winter (December to February) brings colder temperatures and occasional snowfall. While Tallinn's festive holiday atmosphere is charming, this period is ideal for those who enjoy winter activities and a quieter city ambiance.

Regardless of the season, it's advisable to bring layers, a waterproof jacket, and comfortable footwear to adapt to the varying weather conditions. Checking the weather forecast before your trip ensures you pack accordingly and make the most of your time exploring Tallinn's enchanting streets.

Souvenir and Shopping

Exploring Tallinn's diverse shopping scene provides an opportunity to bring back unique souvenirs and gifts. The city's Old Town is a haven for shoppers, featuring a myriad of boutiques, craft shops, and galleries. Consider purchasing traditional Estonian handicrafts, including hand-knit items, wooden toys, and ceramics, as meaningful gifts for friends and family.

Balti Jaama Turg, one of Tallinn's most popular markets, offers a wide array of local products, from fresh produce to handmade crafts. Dive into the vibrant atmosphere and discover Baltic flavors through artisanal cheeses, local honey, and freshly baked bread.

For fashion enthusiasts, Telliskivi Creative City is a trendy area with a mix of vintage shops, designer boutiques, and art studios. Find unique clothing items, accessories, and contemporary art pieces that capture the essence of Tallinn's creative spirit.

Explore Viru Keskus, one of Tallinn's largest shopping centers, for a modern retail experience. Here, you'll find international brands, local designers, and a diverse range of products under one roof. Take advantage of the center's services, including dining options and entertainment facilities.

When selecting souvenirs, prioritize items that reflect Tallinn's cultural identity, such as Vana Tallinn liqueur, traditional marzipan, or locally crafted jewelry. These unique mementos encapsulate the spirit of your Tallinn journey and make for cherished keepsakes.

Navigation and Map

Efficient navigation is essential for making the most of your time in Tallinn. While the city is relatively compact and walkable, having a reliable map enhances your exploration. Begin by obtaining a city map from your accommodation or a local tourist information center.

Digital navigation tools, such as Google Maps, are valuable for real-time directions and information about public transportation options. Download offline maps before your trip to ensure access even without internet connectivity.

Tallinn's well-maintained street signs and clear city layout make it easy to navigate on foot. The Old Town's medieval streets, while charming, can be a bit labyrinthine, so having a map on hand ensures you don't miss any hidden gems.

Consider utilizing public transportation for longer distances or exploring areas outside the city center. Tallinn's buses, trams, and trolleys offer convenient options for reaching various neighborhoods and attractions.

For a more immersive experience, join guided walking tours or use self-guided tour apps to explore Tallinn's historical and cultural landmarks. These tours often provide insightful commentary, enhancing your understanding of the city's rich history.

Popular Markets

Tallinn's markets offer a vibrant beauty of local flavors, crafts, and cultural experiences. Explore these popular markets to immerse yourself in the city's diverse offerings.

Balti Jaama Turg: This market is a treasure trove of fresh produce, local delicacies, and handmade crafts. From traditional Estonian foods to unique souvenirs, it's a must-visit destination for an authentic Tallinn experience.

Telliskivi Loomelinnak (Telliskivi Creative City): While not a traditional market, this creative hub hosts flea markets and pop-up events where you can discover vintage finds, handmade goods, and trendy designer items. The atmosphere is lively, reflecting Tallinn's artistic spirit.

Kalamaja Turg: Located in the trendy Kalamaja district, this market offers a glimpse into local life. Explore stalls filled with fresh produce, artisanal products, and handmade items. It's an excellent place to interact with locals and savor the neighborhood's unique charm.

Rahva Raamat Kirjastus (People's Bookstore): This bookstore, although not a traditional market, is a cultural hub where you can find a wide selection of books, souvenirs, and gifts. It's a great place to explore Tallinn's literary scene and discover works by local authors.

Nõmme Turg: Venture to the suburb of Nõmme to experience a more laid-back market atmosphere. Enjoy browsing through stalls offering fresh produce, flowers, and local crafts. Nõmme Turf provides a tranquil escape from the bustling city center.

Whether you're seeking fresh ingredients, unique souvenirs, or a glimpse into local life, Tallinn's popular markets offer a diverse array of experiences. Take the time to explore these vibrant hubs and uncover the city's dynamic and cultural diversity.

Suggested Itinerary

Embarking on a two-week journey through Tallinn allows for a comprehensive exploration of the city's rich history, cultural landmarks, and vibrant neighborhoods. Tailor your itinerary based on personal interests and preferences, combining must-see attractions with hidden gems for an immersive experience.

Day 1-3: Discover Tallinn's Old Town

Begin your journey in the heart of Tallinn – the Old Town. Explore Toompea Castle, Alexander Nevsky Cathedral, and the medieval Town Hall Square. Wander through cobblestone streets, discovering quaint shops and cozy cafes.

Day 4-5: Art and Creativity in Kalamaja

Head to the trendy Kalamaja district, known for its creative atmosphere. Visit Telliskivi Creative City, exploring art galleries, boutiques, and enjoying local cuisine in the area's hip restaurants. Dive into the unique charm of Seaplane Harbour, a maritime museum housed in historic seaplane hangars.

Day 6-7: Nature and Parks

Escape to nature at Kadriorg Park, home to Kadriorg Palace and the KUMU Art Museum. Stroll through the Japanese Garden and enjoy the serene atmosphere. Explore Pirita Promenade for scenic views of the Baltic Sea and the iconic Tallinn TV Tower.

Day 8-9: Day Trips to Lahemaa National Park

Venture outside Tallinn for a day trip to Lahemaa National Park. Explore diverse landscapes, including forests, bogs, and coastal areas. Visit historic manors like Palmse and Sagadi, and connect with Estonia's natural beauty.

Day 10-11: Tallinn's Culinary Scene

Dive into Tallinn's gastronomy by trying local dishes at Rataskaevu 16 and F-hoone. Explore the Baltic and Scandinavian influences in the city's cuisine. Visit Balti Jaama Turg and local markets to savor authentic flavors.

Day 12-14: Cultural Experiences and Relaxation

Immerse yourself in Tallinn's cultural scene. Attend a performance at the Estonian National Opera or explore the Kumu Art Museum. Take a leisurely stroll through the charming streets of the Lower Town. Wind down your journey with relaxation at a spa or a visit to the city's beaches.

This suggested two-week itinerary offers a balanced mix of historical exploration, artistic encounters, culinary delights, and moments of relaxation. Customize your schedule based on personal preferences, and be open to serendipitous discoveries that make your Tallinn experience truly unique.

Useful Language Phrases

Mastering a few key phrases in Estonian enhances your travel experience in Tallinn and fosters positive interactions with locals. Here are some essential phrases for basic conversations, greetings, numbers 1-10, ordering food, and asking for directions:

Basic Conversations:

1. Hello - Tere
2. Goodbye - Nägemist
3. Thank you - Aitäh
4. Please - Palun
5. Excuse me - Vabandage
6. Yes - Jah
7. No - Ei
8. I don't understand - Ma ei saa aru
9. Can you help me? - Kas saate mind aidata?
10. What is your name? - Mis on teie nimi?

Greetings:

Good morning - Tere hommikust

Good afternoon - Tere päevast

Good evening - Tere õhtust

How are you? - Kuidas sul läheb?

I'm fine, thank you - Mul läheb hästi, aitäh

Numbers 1-10:

One - Üks

Two - Kaks

Three - Kolm

Four - Neli

Five - Viis

Six - Kuus

Seven - Seitse

Eight - Kaheksa

Nine - Üheksa

Ten - Kümme

Ordering Food:

Can I see the menu, please? - Kas ma saaksin menüüd näha, palun?

I would like... - Ma sooviksin...

A table for two, please - Laua kahele, palun

What do you recommend? - Mida te soovitate?

The bill, please - Arve, palun

Directions:

Where is...? - Kus on...?

How do I get to...? - Kuidas ma jõuan...?

Is it far? - Kas see on kaugel?

Left - Vasakule

Right - Paremale

Straight ahead - Otse

Behind - Taga

In front of - Ees

Excuse me, where is the nearest...? - Vabandage, kus on lähim...?

Can you show me on the map? - Kas saate mulle kaardil näidata?

Practice these phrases to feel more comfortable engaging with locals and navigating through Tallinn. Estonians appreciate efforts to speak their language, and even a few basic phrases can go a long way in creating a positive and memorable travel experience.

Chapter Four

Must-See Attractions

Exploring Tallinn unveils stunning historical, cultural, and architectural wonders. The city's rich heritage, well-preserved medieval structures, and vibrant neighborhoods make it a captivating destination. In this chapter, we'll delve into five must-see attractions that showcase the essence of Tallinn's allure.

Tallinn Old Town

Tallinn's Old Town stands as a testament to the city's medieval past, earning it a well-deserved spot on UNESCO's World Heritage List. The enchanting cobblestone streets wind through a maze of well-preserved buildings, revealing centuries of history. Toompea Castle, perched on a limestone hill, overlooks the Lower Town and provides panoramic views of Tallinn's red-tiled rooftops.

Explore the Town Hall Square, a hub of activity surrounded by colorful merchant houses. The Gothic-style Town Hall itself, dating back to the 13th century, is a masterpiece of medieval architecture. Immerse yourself in the unique charm of St. Olaf's Church, once the tallest building in the world. The Alexander Nevsky Cathedral, with its impressive onion domes, is an iconic symbol of Tallinn's skyline.

Kadriorg Palace and Park

Nestled in the Kadriorg district, Kadriorg Palace is a splendid example of Baroque architecture. Commissioned by Peter the Great for his wife Catherine I, the palace now houses the Kadriorg Art Museum, showcasing a diverse collection of foreign art. The surrounding Kadriorg Park, designed in the French formal style, invites leisurely strolls among manicured gardens, fountains, and picturesque pathways.

Seaplane Harbour

Dive into Tallinn's maritime history at the Seaplane Harbour, a unique museum housed in historic seaplane hangars. The highlight is the Lembit submarine, providing insight into Estonia's naval past. Interactive exhibits, including simulators and touchscreens, engage visitors in an immersive exploration of Estonia's maritime heritage. The museum's design, with floating vessels and aircraft suspended from the ceiling, adds a captivating visual dimension to the experience.

Alexander Nevsky Cathedral

The Alexander Nevsky Cathedral, a striking Orthodox masterpiece, graces the Toompea Hill skyline. Built in the late 19th century, this cathedral stands as a symbol of Estonia's complex history. Its impressive domes, intricate mosaics, and ornate interior make it a captivating architectural gem. Visitors are drawn not only to its religious significance but also to the stunning visual impact it contributes to Tallinn's skyline.

Telliskivi Creative City

Venture beyond historical landmarks to the vibrant and creative heart of Tallinn – Telliskivi Creative City. This former industrial complex has been transformed into a hub of artistic expression, housing galleries, studios, shops, and trendy cafes. Explore the street art, attend cultural events, and immerse yourself in the dynamic energy of this alternative cultural district. Telliskivi reflects Tallinn's commitment to both preserving its history and embracing contemporary creativity.

In discovering these must-see attractions, visitors unravel the layers of Tallinn's past and present, gaining a profound appreciation for the city's unique identity. Each site contributes to the narrative of Estonia's capital, creating an unforgettable cultural environment and architectural splendor.

Chapter Five

Top Cities Near Tallinn

Tallinn's strategic location on the shores of the Baltic Sea provides travelers with an opportunity to explore not only Estonia's capital but also its neighboring cities. This chapter delves into ten top cities near Tallinn, each offering a distinctive blend of history, culture, and unique experiences.

Helsinki, Finland

A mere two-hour ferry ride across the Baltic Sea, Helsinki welcomes visitors with its modern architecture, vibrant markets, and a rich cultural scene. Explore iconic landmarks like the Helsinki Cathedral, visit the bustling Senate Square, and indulge in Finnish sauna traditions. The close proximity makes it an ideal day trip destination, forging a unique connection between the two capital cities.

Riga, Latvia

Embark on a journey south to discover Riga, Latvia's charming capital, just a four-hour drive from Tallinn. Riga's Old Town, a UNESCO World Heritage site, captivates with its medieval architecture, cobblestone streets, and lively atmosphere. Explore the Freedom Monument, stroll along the Daugava River, and savor Latvian cuisine in this city where history seamlessly blends with modern vitality.

St. Petersburg, Russia

Approximately five hours east of Tallinn, St. Petersburg beckons with its opulent palaces, world-class museums, and the iconic Hermitage. Marvel at the grandeur of the Winter Palace, immerse yourself in Russian art at the State Russian Museum, and cruise along the picturesque canals. St. Petersburg's cultural richness and architectural splendor make it a captivating destination for those willing to venture beyond Tallinn.

Stockholm, Sweden

A comfortable ferry ride across the Baltic Sea brings travelers to Stockholm, a city spread across 14 islands. The Swedish capital boasts a maritime charm, with historic districts like Gamla Stan and modern attractions such as the Vasa Museum. Explore the Royal Palace, stroll along the scenic waterfront, and savor Swedish delicacies. Stockholm's unique blend of history, culture, and natural beauty invites a memorable exploration from Tallinn.

Vilnius, Lithuania

Heading south, Vilnius, Lithuania's capital, awaits approximately four hours from Tallinn. Vilnius enchants with its Baroque architecture, vibrant arts scene, and a UNESCO-listed Old Town. Discover the Hill of Crosses, visit the Gediminas Castle, and immerse yourself in the city's creative spirit. Vilnius, often called the "Jerusalem of the North," invites exploration into its cultural heritage and modern vitality.

Turku, Finland

Venture westward to Turku, Finland's oldest city and an architectural gem situated at the mouth of the Aura River. A four-hour drive from Tallinn, Turku's medieval castle, picturesque archipelago, and vibrant cultural events make it a delightful destination. Explore the Turku Archipelago, visit the Turku Castle, and experience the city's maritime heritage, offering a refreshing contrast to Tallinn's historical charm.

Tartu, Estonia

A shorter journey south brings travelers to Tartu, Estonia's second-largest city. Rich in history and intellectual culture, Tartu boasts the University of Tartu, Estonia's oldest university. Wander through the Old Town, visit the Estonian National Museum, and embrace the city's youthful energy. Tartu offers a unique blend of tradition and innovation, providing a captivating experience for those exploring beyond Tallinn's borders.

Pärnu, Estonia

Westward lies Pärnu, Estonia's summer capital, nestled along the scenic coastline of the Gulf of Riga. A two-hour drive from Tallinn, Pärnu is renowned for its sandy beaches, historic architecture, and vibrant spa culture. Explore the Pärnu Old Town, rejuvenate in a seaside spa, and enjoy the relaxed atmosphere of this coastal gem, offering a serene escape from the bustling energy of the capital.

Kaunas, Lithuania

Journey south to Kaunas, Lithuania's second-largest city and a hub of historical significance. Approximately four hours from Tallinn, Kaunas features architectural wonders, including the Gothic-style Kaunas Castle and the Pazaislis Monastery. Explore the Old Town, stroll along the Nemunas River, and witness the city's transformation into a modern cultural center. Kaunas invites travelers to discover Lithuania's diverse heritage and contemporary vibrancy.

Narva, Estonia

To the east, close to the Russian border, sits Narva, a city rich in history and cultural diversity. Narva, a three-hour journey from Tallinn, is known for its majestic Hermann

Castle and unique blend of Estonian and Russian elements. Visit the Narva Museum, walk along the Narva River, and take in the varied landscapes that distinguish this border city. Narva provides a look of Estonia's diverse past and intriguing present.

These ten cities around Tallinn provide a diverse tapestry of cultures, history, and landscapes, encouraging visitors to venture beyond Estonia's capital. Each stop adds a new chapter to the Baltic story, guaranteeing a diverse and enriching experience for visitors keen to discover the gems surrounding Tallinn.

Chapter Six

The Top Hidden Gems

Kalamaja District

Nestled just west of Tallinn's Old Town, the Kalamaja quarter is a treasure trove of artistic expression and local charm. Wander through the colorful alleyways covered with street art to find secret courtyards filled with galleries, boutiques, and comfortable cafes. Telliskivi Creative City, an industrial complex transformed into a cultural hub, serves as a focal point for innovation. Experience the creative spirit of local artists, indulge in handmade delights, and appreciate the bohemian vibe that defines this hidden gem.

Estonian Maritime Museum

Located in the ancient Seaplane Harbour, the Estonian Maritime Museum is a hidden jewel that immerses visitors in the country's maritime heritage. The museum, housed in real seaplane hangars, displays an extraordinary collection of nautical items, including historical vessels and interactive exhibitions. The highlight is the Lembit submarine, which provides an intriguing peek into Estonia's naval history. Discover nautical adventures, learn about ship engineering, and understand how the sea shaped Estonia's identity. The museum's distinctive setting and fascinating exhibitions make it an intriguing and lesser-known attraction in Tallinn.

St. Bridget's Convent Ruins

The remnants of St. Bridget's Convent, nestled near Pirita, serve as a haunting reminder of medieval Estonia. This hidden gem offers tourists the chance to explore the remnants of a 15th-century monastery, where traces of history can be heard among the mossy stones.

Wander amid the atmospheric remains, remembering the convent's former magnificence, and find the ancient chapel with its magnificent archways. The adjacent park provides a peaceful escape, allowing visitors to meditate on the passage of time while immersed in nature. St. Bridget's Convent Ruins provide a peaceful getaway from the city while also serving as a melancholy reminder of Estonia's medieval heritage.

Nõmme Market

Travel southwest to the lovely suburb of Nõmme, where the Nõmme Market is a hidden gem offering local cuisines and community spirit. The market, surrounded by ancient buildings, offers a delectable selection of fresh produce, handmade crafts, and traditional Estonian fare. Engage with local sellers, smell the aroma of freshly baked bread, and browse the stalls selling homemade products. Nõmme Market offers a genuine peek into suburban life, with a slow pace and strong community connections. This hidden gem takes a break from the norm, allowing visitors to feel the true warmth and genuineness of Estonian daily life.

Kumu Art Museum

The Kumu Art Museum, located within the Kadriorg Palace complex, is a hidden gem dedicated to Estonia's artistic past. Kumu, Estonia's largest art museum, is modern and energetic, with a broad collection of Estonian art ranging from the 18th to contemporary works. The museum's architectural design blends smoothly with the historic surroundings, resulting in a harmonious environment for artistic discovery. Wander through thought-provoking exhibitions, learn about the growth of Estonian art, and admire the new viewpoints offered by local and international artists. Kumu Art Museum is a cultural refuge that welcomes visitors to explore Estonia's artistic history while enjoying the tranquil ambiance of Kadriorg Park, which surrounds this hidden jewel.

Chapter Seven

Accommodation Options

When planning a trip to Tallinn, selecting the correct accommodations is critical to ensure a comfortable and enjoyable stay. This chapter investigates a variety of options, from upscale hotels and resorts to low-cost accommodations, providing insights into the different options available to all types of travelers.

Hotel and Resort

Tallinn has a plethora of hotels and resorts that cater to discerning guests seeking elegance, comfort, and first-rate services. The historic center of the city, particularly around Old Town and Toompea, is home to various luxury institutions that offer a mix of modern sophistication and old charm.

Luxurious hotels, such as the Telegraaf Hotel, located in a 19th-century telegraph building, offer an indulgent experience with nicely appointed rooms, great cuisine, and spa services. The Hotel Schlossle, a member of the esteemed Relais and Châteaux, combines historic ambiance with individual service to provide a genuinely luxurious experience.

For those looking for a resort experience close to Tallinn, the Tallinn Viimsi Spa and Water Park offers a haven of leisure. This resort, located on the banks of the Baltic Sea, provides spa services, a water park, and spectacular sea views.

Furthermore, worldwide hotel chains such as Hilton Tallinn Park and Radisson Blu Hotel Olümpia offer a perfect blend of international standards and Estonian hospitality. These places frequently provide modern facilities, rooftop bars, and panoramic views of the city.

Low Budget Accommodations

Tallinn offers a wide range of economical and inviting lodging options for budget travelers. Hostels, guesthouses, and low-cost hotels are spread around the city, providing comfort without breaking the bank.

The Telliskivi Creative City region is not just a cultural hub, but also a popular destination for low-cost accommodations. Hostels such as The Monk's Bunk Hostel and Red Emperor Hostel offer a friendly atmosphere and easy access to nearby attractions. These lodgings frequently include social areas, kitchen facilities, and organized events, which fosters a sense of community among guests.

Kalamaja and Kristiine provide a variety of budget-friendly motels with a touch of local flavor. The Baltic Hotel Vana Wiru, located in the Old Town, offers reasonable rooms without compromising on location or comfort. The

Economy Hotel, located near the train station, is another inexpensive option for guests that value accessibility.

Tallinn has an abundance of apartments and guesthouses for individuals who desire a more independent and self-catering experience. Platforms like Airbnb provide a variety of low-cost options, allowing tourists to stay in residential neighborhoods and see Tallinn like a local.

Furthermore, Tallinn Backpackers, located in the center of the Old Town, is a popular option for budget-conscious guests. This hostel not only provides affordable lodging but also organizes activities that allow guests to connect with other travelers.

Regardless of budget, Tallinn ensures that every guest can find appropriate lodging. Whether you choose a fancy hotel with spectacular city views or a quiet hostel in a creative sector, Tallinn's accommodation options add to the city's overall charm by catering to a wide range of preferences and making each stay unique.

Unique Accommodation

Tallinn provides more than just a place to stay, with a variety of unique accommodation experiences that contribute to the attractiveness of the visit. These unique possibilities offer not only pleasant accommodations, but also the ability to immerse oneself in the city's history, culture, and creativity.

One such option is to stay at a boutique hotel inside Tallinn's historic walls. The Three Sisters Hotel, housed in three wonderfully maintained merchant houses, takes guests to a bygone period with antique furnishings and a historical atmosphere. Similarly, the Merchants House Hotel, located in a

14th-century structure, provides an intimate and authentic Tallinn experience.

For a more whimsical stay, consider the Schlössle Hotel, a boutique hotel housed in a 13th-century structure with a beautiful courtyard. Its distinctive decor and attention to detail create an appealing ambiance that reflects Tallinn's fairy-tale charm.

Tallinn also has a number of themed hotels in addition to traditional ones. The CRU Hotel, for example, is well-known for its theatrical motif, which immerses visitors in a milieu inspired by the world of theater and drama. Each room is designed to evoke a distinct play or era, resulting in a genuinely unique and immersive visit.

For nature lovers, the Vihula Manor Country Club and Spa, located just outside Tallinn, provides a tranquil refuge. Set in verdant countryside, this mansion offers a natural respite while being close to the city. Guests can relax in the spa, explore the manor's park, and live the Estonian country life.

Booking Tip and Recommendations

Booking the ideal hotel in Tallinn necessitates careful planning and consideration of individual preferences. Here are some suggestions to ensure a successful booking experience:

Book in Advance: It is recommended that you book your accommodations well in advance, especially during busy tourist seasons. This not only ensures availability, but may also result in lower rates.

Consider Location: Select accommodations based on your planned activities. Staying within the ancient walls is convenient if you want to explore the Old Town. For those looking for a more local experience, Kalamaja and Telliskivi Creative City offer a vibrant and authentic ambiance.

Read Reviews: Before making a reservation, read reviews from other travelers on websites such as TripAdvisor, Booking.com, and Google Reviews. Previous guests' feedback provides vital insights into service quality, cleanliness, and overall contentment.

Budget Considerations: Set a budget for your hotel, taking into account amenities, location, and length of stay. Be flexible with your dates to take advantage of any potential discounts or special deals.

Consider unique lodging options for a memorable visit. Boutique hotels, themed lodgings, and stays in historic buildings provide a unique perspective on Tallinn's beauty.

Check Cancellation Policies: Before finalizing a reservation, carefully read the cancellation policy. Choose accommodations that provide flexible cancellation policies, allowing you to change your plans as needed.

Look for Package packages: Some lodgings have package packages that include extra facilities or services. Explore these choices to improve your stay while perhaps saving money overall.

Use reward Programs: If you frequently stay with the same hotel chain, consider joining their reward program. This could result in incentives like room upgrades, discounts, or more amenities.

Confirm Inclusions: Determine what is included in the room rate. Some motels provide free breakfast, Wi-Fi, or access to wellness centers. Knowing what is included assists in determining the total value.

Contact Directly: If you have specific requirements or questions, please contact the accommodation directly. This promotes clear communication and may result in personalized recommendations or unique arrangements.

By carefully considering these ideas and recommendations, tourists may traverse Tallinn's broad hotel scene, making informed decisions that match their preferences and improve their entire experience.

Chapter Eight

Transportation System and Cautions

Public Transportation Overview

Using Tallinn's public transit system is a quick and easy method to explore the city and its surroundings. The well-organized network includes buses, trams, trolleys, and even ferries, giving inhabitants and visitors a variety of options for getting around.

Buses and Trolleys: Tallinn's bus and trolleybus system serves the entire city, including the central and suburban areas. The vehicles are modern, well-maintained, and come with dependable schedules. The central bus terminal, located near the Old Town, acts as a significant hub for several routes.

Travelers can buy tickets directly from the driver or use the contactless smartcard system for a smoother travel.

Trams: Tallinn's tram system is another important mode of public transportation, providing a scenic and quick means to get around the city. Tram lines connect significant districts, such as Old Town, Kadriorg, and the waterfront. Trams are a popular mode of transportation for individuals who want to take in the sights of the city.

Consider using the Tallinn Card to make public transportation more convenient. This comprehensive city card offers unlimited access to buses, trolleys, and trams for a set period of time. It also provides free admission to many destinations, making it a budget-friendly alternative for both transit and tourism.

Renting A Vehicle

While Tallinn's public transportation is extensive, renting a vehicle provides flexibility and the opportunity to explore the city and its surroundings at one's leisure. Here's a guide for hiring a vehicle in Tallinn:

automobile Rentals: Tallinn has several international and local automobile rental firms. Rental offices are located at Tallinn Airport and in the city center, providing a convenient experience for flight travelers. Popular worldwide brands like Hertz, Avis, and Europcar, as well as local businesses like Budget and Sixt, provide a variety of automobile options.

Documentation: To rent a car in Tallinn, you will normally need a valid driver's license, passport, and credit card. It is best to check the exact requirements of the rental company you choose.

Road Network: Estonia has a well-maintained road network, and driving in and around Tallinn is simple. Drivers can easily navigate the city because of its well-marked roads and contemporary infrastructure. However, be aware of local traffic laws and restrictions.

Parking: Tallinn has both street parking and parking lots. The Old Town has little parking, so it's best to park in approved spots. Some regions may require payment for parking, and it is customary to use a parking app or buy a parking card.

Caution: While renting a vehicle is convenient, there are some things to consider. Tallinn encounters cold weather, and driving conditions can be difficult. Ensure that the rental car is equipped with adequate winter tires. Also, be aware of wildlife, especially in rural regions.

Gas Stations: There are plenty of gas stations in Estonia, and most people pay with credit cards. It is advisable to refuel before going on lengthy excursions, especially if visiting rural or sparsely populated areas.

Public Transport and Car Rental: For a more balanced approach, some travelers choose public transportation within Tallinn and car rental for day trips or touring more outlying areas. This provides visitors with the convenience of both alternatives.

Whether you use Tallinn's excellent public transportation or rent a car, knowing your options and taking the required measures assures a smooth and enjoyable exploration of the city and its surroundings.

Precautions for Travelers

While Tallinn is a relatively safe location, as with any other city, travelers must take some steps to ensure a smooth and secure stay. Here are some precautionary steps for tourists visiting Tallinn:

Pickpocketing: Exercise caution in crowded settings, particularly popular tourist destinations and public transit. Keep valuables safe, utilize anti-theft bags, and remain mindful of your surroundings.

Street Safety: While Tallinn is typically safe, it is prudent to exercise caution at night, particularly in less busy or poorly illuminated areas. Stay on well-traveled roads and choose trustworthy transit choices.

Traffic Awareness: When taking public transportation, be aware of traffic, especially when crossing streets. Follow traffic laws and utilize authorized crosswalks. When renting a vehicle, follow local driving laws and be mindful of potential hazards.

Winter Weather Precautions: Tallinn has cold winters, and snow and ice can provide slick conditions. Wear adequate footwear, exercise caution on ice surfaces, and take public transportation or taxis if driving conditions become difficult.

Emergency Numbers: Learn the local emergency numbers, such as police and medical services, as well as the contact information for your country's embassy or consulate. Keep a copy of important documents, like your passport, apart from the originals.

Health Precautions: Make sure you have travel insurance that includes medical emergencies. Be mindful of your health, particularly during extreme weather conditions. Learn the locations of neighboring medical facilities.

Cultural Respect: Estonia has a distinct culture, and it is critical to respect local customs and traditions. Dress modestly while visiting holy sites, seek permission before photographing residents, and be mindful of cultural sensitivities.

Internet Security: When utilizing public Wi-Fi, avoid sharing important information. Use virtual private networks (VPNs) to increase security. Avoid accessing critical accounts from public computers.

Nature Caution: When exploring natural regions or parks, adopt safety precautions. Respect wildlife, follow indicated pathways, and be aware of changing weather conditions.

Travel warnings: Be aware of any travel warnings or updates for Tallinn. Check government sources and diplomatic websites for the most up-to-date information on safety and security.

By taking these precautions, visitors can improve their safety and well-being while experiencing Tallinn. Being aware of the local surroundings, appreciating cultural differences, and being informed all contribute to a happy and safe travel experience in this attractive Baltic metropolis.

Chapter Nine

Top Beaches

Tallinn, recognized for its rich history and medieval beauty, also has lovely beaches that are a refreshing respite for both inhabitants and tourists. This chapter focuses on the top five beaches in and around Tallinn, highlighting the city's diverse coastal scenery.

Pirita Beach

Pirita Beach, located near Tallinn's city center, is a popular and easily accessible coastal location. Stretching along the Pirita River and the Gulf of Finland, this sandy beach provides a magnificent location for leisure and recreation. The soft sands invite beachgoers to relax and enjoy the view of the sea, while the shallow waters are ideal for swimming.

Pirita Beach is a popular destination for water sports enthusiasts as well as sunbathers. Windsurfing and sailing are popular hobbies, and the beach organizes a variety of water sports events all year. The surrounding Pirita promenade is ideal for leisurely strolls, with spectacular views of Tallinn's skyline and the old Pirita Convent.

Pirita has beach volleyball courts, playgrounds, and specific picnic spots for those who want to spend their day at the beach more actively. The beach is easily accessible via public transit, making it a popular location for both locals and tourists.

Stroomi Beach

Stroomi Beach, located in the Pelguranna area, offers a more relaxed and family-friendly environment. This sandy beach spans along the Gulf of Finland, providing a peaceful respite from the city buzz. The shallow waters make it a perfect location for families with children, as they provide a safe atmosphere for swimming and aquatic activities.

The beach is bordered by a park, which makes it a popular location for picnics and outdoor events. Stroomi Beach has good facilities, such as changing rooms, playgrounds, and beach volleyball courts. The scenic walking pathways along the coast provide spectacular views of the water, creating a relaxing atmosphere for visitors.

Stroomi Beach is easily accessible via public transit, and its proximity to the city center makes it an ideal location for a day by the sea. Stroomi Beach is a popular resort for locals looking for a calm getaway.

Kakumäe Beach

Kakumäe Beach, located slightly further from the city center, offers a scenic seaside escape.

Nestled in the Kakumäe area, this beach offers a more private and natural setting. The sandy shoreline, bordered by pine forests, offer a peaceful ambiance for beachgoers seeking tranquility.

Kakumäe Beach is well-known for its clean seas, making it a popular swimming and sunbathing destination. The beach is less congested than some of the more central sites, making it an ideal place to relax. The scenic surroundings make it an ideal location for nature lovers, while the neighboring Kakumäe promenade provides breathtaking views of the sea.

In addition to its natural beauty, Kakumäe Beach attracts water sports enthusiasts. Kayaking and paddleboarding are popular pastimes, and the beach offers boat storage. The Kakumäe Marina contributes to the maritime beauty, resulting in an ideal combination of coastal leisure and recreational activities.

Pikakari Beach

For those looking for a less crowded beach experience, Pikakari Beach is a hidden gem on the Viimsi Peninsula. Nestled along the scenic Pikakari Bay, this pebble beach offers a tranquil environment surrounded by thick flora. The rocky coastline gives a distinct character to the scenery, providing a peaceful respite from the hustle and bustle of city life.

Pikakari Beach is popular with locals searching for a peaceful retreat, and it is generally less congested than some of the more central beaches. The tranquil seas make it ideal for swimming, and the sheltered spots along the shoreline provide the perfect setting for a quiet beach day.

The beach is easily accessible by automobile or public transit, and its proximity to the Viimsi Open Air Museum allows visitors to learn about the region's culture and history. Pikakari Beach is great for those wanting a more private and nature-inspired seaside experience.

Rohuneeme Beach

Rohuneeme Beach, located on the northeastern tip of the Viimsi Peninsula, offers breathtaking coastal views of the Gulf of Finland. This sandy beach, bordered by pine forests and coastal meadows, is an ideal destination for nature lovers and beachgoers.

Rohuneeme Beach is recognized for its clean, shallow waters, making it ideal for both swimming and wading. The broad sandy shores provide plenty of area for sunbathing, picnicking, and beach games. The beach is well-kept, with amenities such as changing rooms and restrooms available to guests.

Rohuneeme Beach is known for its lovely walking routes that extend to the peninsula's tip. Visitors can enjoy spectacular views of the sea and, on clear days, see the adjacent islands. The beach also offers a wonderful vantage point for watching the dawn or sunset, creating a magical ambiance for those looking for a romantic or meditative beach vacation.

Rohuneeme Beach is popular with locals who admire its natural beauty and peacefulness. The neighboring coastal sceneries provide chances for birdwatching, and the nearby Rohuneeme Harbor contributes to the area's marine attractiveness.

In summary, Tallinn's beaches appeal to a wide range of interests, from the crowded Pirita Beach, which offers water sports, to the calm and family-friendly Stroomi Beach. Kakumäe Beach provides a hidden natural hideaway, whereas Pikakari Beach gives a more tranquil coastline respite. Rohuneeme Beach, with its panoramic views and quiet atmosphere, rounds up the top five beaches in and around Tallinn, inviting both locals and visitors to enjoy the numerous coastal amenities of this Baltic treasure.

Chapter Ten

Cultural Experiences

Tallinn, with its rich history and active culture, provides a wide range of experiences beyond its gorgeous architecture and picturesque landscapes. This chapter digs into the cultural and other experiences that make Tallinn such an appealing location.

Local Festivities and Events

Tallinn organizes a number of festivals and events throughout the year, giving visitors a unique opportunity to immerse themselves in the city's cultural energy. These events highlight local customs, arts, and entertainment, providing memorable experiences for both locals and visitors.

Tallinn Music Week, a highlight of the city's cultural calendar, brings together musicians, artists, and music fans from all over the world. The festival offers a wide variety of events, including concerts, workshops, and professional conferences, making it a must-see event for music fans.

The Black Nights Film Festival (PÖFF), held every November, is one of the largest film festivals in Northern Europe. It features a diverse selection of international and local films, bringing together creators, actors, and cinephiles. The festival's wide lineup comprises feature films, documentaries, and animations, offering a cinematic experience to suit all interests.

Tallinn Old Town Days: This yearly celebration takes tourists back in time, providing a look into Tallinn's medieval history. The Old Town Days include reenactments, medieval marketplaces, and traditional entertainment, resulting in an immersive experience that brings the city's history alive.

Christmas Markets: Tallinn's stunning Christmas markets convert the city into a wintry paradise over the holidays. The main market in Old Town's Raekoja Plats sells local crafts, holiday decorations, and a variety of seasonal snacks. The magnificent ambiance, complete with dazzling lights and holiday happiness, draws both locals and tourists.

Participating in these local festivals and events offers a unique opportunity to engage with Tallinn's culture and community, resulting in lasting memories and a better understanding of the city's identity.

Historic and Cultural Tours

Exploring Tallinn's history and cultural heritage is best done on interesting excursions that provide insight into the city's past and present. Various guided excursions provide an in-depth overview of Tallinn's history, architectural marvels, and cultural nuances.

Walking tours of Tallinn's UNESCO-listed Old Town take visitors on a trip through centuries of history. Guided walking tours take guests through cobblestone streets, historical squares, and prominent monuments such as Toompea Castle and Alexander Nevsky Cathedral. Knowledgeable guides tell stories about the city's medieval history and importance in Northern European trade.

Kadriorg Palace and Art Museum Tour: This baroque masterpiece is encircled by the lovely Kadriorg Park. Guided tours of the palace highlight its beautiful interiors and provide information about its past as a dwelling for Russian monarchs. The neighboring Kadriorg Art Museum houses a remarkable collection of foreign art, which adds an artistic element to the journey.

Soviet-era Tallinn Tour: Learn about Tallinn's more recent history with a tour centered on its Soviet past. Explore the remains of Soviet architecture, including the TV Tower and the abandoned Patarei Prison. Guides provide insights into Soviet life, giving visitors a unique view of the city's recent history.

Literary Tallinn Tour: Tallinn has a long literary history, and this tour brings guests to the city's literary icons. Visit landmarks linked with notable Estonian writers, learn about the country's literary heritage, and browse bookshops showcasing Estonia's thriving literary industry.

Food and Culinary excursions: Tallinn's culinary scene reflects its many influences, and food excursions allow tourists to fully experience the city's delicacies. Explore local markets, sample traditional Estonian cuisine, and find culinary jewels.

Participating in historical and cultural tours not only enhances the overall vacation experience, but also builds a stronger connection to Tallinn's legacy. Whether meandering around the medieval Old Town, examining Soviet-era ruins, or sampling local food, these trips offer a nuanced perspective of the city's cultural scenes and activities.

Special Experiences for Travelers

Beyond the well-trodden routes of historical tours and traditional festivals, Tallinn provides one-of-a-kind and eccentric experiences that lend a personal touch to one's visit. These unusual interactions provide travelers unique perspectives on the city's culture and character.

Seaplane Harbour's Maritime Adventure: Visit the Seaplane Harbour to learn about Tallinn's maritime heritage. This interactive museum features a large collection of old seaplanes, submarines, and nautical artifacts. A unique feature is the ability to ride in a flight simulator, which provides an exciting feeling of taking control of an aircraft.

Tallinn TV Tower's Skywalk: For the daring tourist, the Tallinn TV Tower provides a 175-meter-high Skywalk. This open-air platform allows you to walk along the edge of the tower's roof, offering amazing views over the city and its surroundings. It's an amazing experience for individuals who want an adrenaline rush paired with breathtaking landscapes.

Medieval Dining Experience: Immerse yourself in medieval history by dining in Tallinn's Old Town. Several restaurants provide medieval-themed meals where visitors can eat traditional foods while being served by dressed staff in a period-appropriate setting. It's a lovely way to experience the flavors and atmosphere of medieval Tallinn.

KUMU Art Museum Night Tour: Take a night tour of the KUMU Art Museum to see art from a different perspective. This contemporary art museum, constructed as a blend of modern buildings and natural settings, has a distinct ambiance after sunset. The guided night tour allows for an intimate investigation of the museum's displays, with special lighting creating an intriguing atmosphere.

Discover Estonia's digital capabilities by visiting the e-Estonia Showroom. This creative venue demonstrates the country's e-governance solutions, digital infrastructure, and the impact of technology on Estonian society. It's an eye-opening event for anyone interested in the convergence of culture and technology.

These one-of-a-kind experiences allow visitors to discover Tallinn from a variety of perspectives, such as soaring above the city on a Skywalk, dining like medieval royalty, or exploring the digital advancements that define modern Estonia. These unexpected encounters add to a well-rounded and enjoyable tour of Tallinn's cultural kaleidoscope.

Chapter Eleven

Useful Tips for Tourists and Travelers

Visiting Tallinn is a wonderful journey, and having practical ideas and insights can help make the experience go smoothly and pleasurable. This chapter provides a thorough collection of valuable suggestions for tourists and travelers visiting Estonia's attractive capital.

Currency and Payment

Estonia has the Euro (EUR) as its official currency. Major credit and debit cards are commonly accepted in Tallinn, particularly in hotels, restaurants, and bigger retail outlets. However, it is recommended that you bring some cash with you to smaller establishments and markets.

Language

The official language is Estonian, but English is frequently used, especially in tourist areas, hotels, and restaurants. Most residents working in the tourism industry are fluent in English, making communication reasonably simple for English-speaking visitors.

Public Transport

Tallinn's public transportation network, which includes buses, trams, and trolleys, is efficient and well-connected. Consider obtaining the Tallinn Card, which grants unrestricted access to public transportation and free admission to a variety of sites. It's an inexpensive way to experience the city.

Walk Tours

Tallinn's Old Town is ideal for walking tours due to its tiny size. A guided walking tour is a great opportunity to learn about the city's history and find hidden treasures. The cobblestone streets can be uneven, so wear comfortable shoes.

Weather Considerations

Estonia has distinct seasons. Summers are moderate, and winters can be cold with snowfall. Check the weather prediction prior to your journey and pack accordingly. In the winter, prepare for icy conditions, while in the summer, bring clothing for colder evenings.

Internet Connectivity

Tallinn has great internet connectivity, with free Wi-Fi available in many public areas, hotels, and cafes. Consider buying a local SIM card for your phone to ensure reliable internet access while visiting the city.

Safety

Tallinn is generally considered a safe place for travelers. Maintain normal measures, such as keeping an eye on your valuables in crowded situations. The Old Town can get crowded, so be wary of pickpockets. Dial 112 to access emergency services.

Open Hours

Shops, particularly in the Old Town, may have varying operating hours. The majority of museums and attractions have set hours of operation, so check ahead of time. Plan your visits carefully, especially if you have limited time.

Local Cuisine

Estonian cuisine is eclectic, drawing from Nordic, Russian, and German traditions. Local cuisines include (potato porridge), herring, and black bread. Do not miss out on the marinated sprats, a Baltic delicacy.

Tap Water

The tap water in Tallinn is safe to drink. You may refill your reusable water bottle with confidence throughout your vacation, saving money and the environment.

Sunset on Toompea Hill

Toompea Hill offers a spectacular view in the evening. The sunset over the city from this elevated vantage is beautiful. Bring your camera to capture the magnificent hues of the sunset.

Day Trips

Consider day visits to local attractions like Lahemaa National Park, Paldiski, and Haapsalu. Estonia's tiny size makes it easy to explore beyond the city borders.

Estonian Saunas

Experience traditional Estonian saunas. Many hotels and spas provide saunas, which provide a calming and culturally absorbing experience.

Local Event Calendar

Check the local events calendar for festivals, concerts, and other special events scheduled during your visit. Participating in local celebrations might provide you with a unique cultural experience.

Photo Etiquette

When photographing locals, remember to respect their privacy and cultural traditions. Ask for permission before photographing people, especially in more intimate or home circumstances.

Emergency Service

Know the following emergency numbers: 112 for general emergencies, 110 for police, and 113 for medical aid.

Tipping Etiquette

While service costs are frequently included on bills, it is usual to round up or give a little tip for excellent service at restaurants. Tipping is also customary in taxis and with tour guides.

Cultural Sensitivity

Show respect for local customs and traditions. When visiting holy sites, dress modestly and consider cultural sensitivity.

Local Markets

Explore local markets like Balti Jaama Turg to get a sense of Estonian culture. These markets provide fresh vegetables, homemade products, and the opportunity to interact with locals.

Pack Accordingly

Pack necessities such as good walking shoes, weather-appropriate clothing, a power adaptor, and any special prescriptions or personal items you may require.

With these helpful ideas, you'll be well-prepared to make the most of your time in Tallinn. Whether you're enjoying local cuisine, visiting historical monuments, or admiring the city's beauty, these tips will help you make the most of your trip to Estonia's lovely capital.

Chapter Twelve

Other Resources

When planning a trip to Tallinn, having access to a variety of resources can enhance your travel experience, making it smoother and more enjoyable. This chapter provides an extensive list of additional resources, including travel apps, websites, guidebooks, and local services that can help you navigate Tallinn like a pro. Whether you're looking for the best transportation options, cultural insights, or emergency contacts, these resources will be invaluable.

Travel Apps for Exploring Tallinn

In the digital age, travel apps have become indispensable tools for travelers. Here are some highly recommended apps that can help you during your stay in Tallinn:

- Google Maps: Essential for navigation, Google Maps provides detailed maps, directions, and information on public transportation routes in Tallinn. It also offers reviews and ratings for local businesses and attractions.

- Citymapper: This app is excellent for navigating Tallinn's public transportation system. It provides real-time updates, route planning, and timetables for buses, trams, and trains.

- TripAdvisor: Use TripAdvisor to read reviews, find the best restaurants, hotels, and attractions in Tallinn. The app also allows you to book tours and activities directly.

- Uber/Bolt: For convenient transportation options, both Uber and Bolt (originally an Estonian company) operate in Tallinn, offering reliable ride-hailing services.

- Google Translate: Although many Estonians speak English, having Google Translate can be helpful for translating signs, menus, and conversations.

Essential Websites for Tallinn Visitors

Several websites provide comprehensive information about Tallinn, catering to various aspects of travel planning:

- Visit Tallinn (visittallinn.ee): The official tourism website for Tallinn, offering detailed information on attractions, events, accommodation, dining, and more. It's a great starting point for planning your trip.

- Estonian Tourist Board (visitestonia.com): This site provides broader information on traveling in Estonia, including Tallinn. It covers various travel tips, cultural insights, and regional highlights.

- Tallinn Card (tallinncard.ee): Learn about the benefits of the Tallinn Card, which offers free or discounted entry to numerous attractions, museums, and public transportation.

- E-Estonia (e-estonia.com): For those interested in Estonia's digital advancements, this site offers insights into the country's innovative e-governance and digital society initiatives.

Local Services and Contacts

Having access to local services and emergency contacts can be crucial during your travels. Here are some important resources to keep in mind:

- Emergency Numbers: In case of emergencies, dial 112 for police, fire, and medical services.

- Embassies and Consulates: Locate the nearest embassy or consulate for your country. The

U.S. Embassy in Tallinn, for example, can be found at Kentmanni 20, 15099 Tallinn, Estonia (website: ee.usembassy.gov).

- Tourist Information Centers: The main Tourist Information Center is located at Niguliste 2, 10146 Tallinn, Estonia. They offer maps, brochures, and assistance for tourists.

- Pharmacies and Medical Assistance: Pharmacies are widely available in Tallinn, with many open 24/7. For medical assistance, North Estonia Medical Centre (PERH) is one of the major hospitals.

Cultural and Historical Resources

Understanding the cultural and historical context of Tallinn can enrich your travel experience. Here are some resources to explore:

- Estonian National Museum (ERM): Located in Tartu, this museum provides a comprehensive overview of Estonian culture and history. Their website offers online exhibits and resources (erm.ee).

- Tallinn City Museum: This museum provides insights into the history and development of Tallinn. It's a great place to start your exploration of the city's past (linnamuuseum.ee).

- Books on Estonian History: Consider reading books such as "The Baltic: A History" by Michael North and "Estonia: A Modern History" by Neil Taylor for a deeper understanding of the region's history.

Social Media and Online Communities

Engaging with online communities can provide real-time tips and advice from fellow travelers and locals:

- Facebook Groups: Join groups like "Tallinn Expats and Locals" or "Tallinn Travel Tips" to connect with other travelers and residents.

- Instagram: Follow hashtags like VisitTallinn, TallinnFood, and TallinnOldTown to discover hidden gems and popular spots through the eyes of other visitors.

- Reddit: The r/Estonia subreddit is a valuable resource for asking questions, sharing experiences, and getting advice from locals and travelers.

Educational and Entertainment Resources

Learn more about Estonia and Tallinn through documentaries, films, and online courses:

- Documentaries: Watch documentaries such as "The Singing Revolution" to understand Estonia's path to independence.

- Films: Enjoy Estonian cinema with films like "Tangerines" and "November," which offer a glimpse into the country's culture and storytelling.

- Online Courses: Platforms like Coursera and Udemy offer courses on Estonian history, culture, and even language lessons to enhance your travel experience.

Sustainable Travel Resources

For environmentally conscious travelers, here are resources to help you make sustainable choices:

- Eco-Estonia (ecoestonia.com): This website provides information on eco-friendly travel options, including green accommodation, sustainable dining, and responsible tourism practices.

- Green Key Hotels: Look for Green Key-certified hotels in Tallinn, which adhere to strict environmental standards (greenkey.global).

Access to a variety of resources can significantly enhance your travel experience in Tallinn. Whether you prefer digital tools, traditional guidebooks, or community engagement, the information provided in this chapter will help you navigate the city with confidence and make the most of your visit.

Bus Lines in Tallinn

Tallinn boasts a comprehensive and efficient public bus system, which is an integral part of the city's public transportation network. Managed by Tallinna Linnatranspordi AS, the buses provide extensive coverage across the city and its surrounding areas. This makes it an accessible and convenient mode of transport for both locals and visitors.

Where to Find Bus Lines

Bus Stops and Stations:

- City Center (Viru Keskus): One of the main hubs, Viru Keskus, is located in the heart of Tallinn and connects several major bus lines. It's easily accessible and a great starting point for many journeys.

- Balti Jaam: This central railway station is also a significant bus stop, providing connections to various parts of the city.

- Lasnamäe and Mustamäe: These residential districts have numerous bus stops that serve the local population and visitors staying in these areas.

Online Resources and Apps:

- Tallinn Transport Website (transport.tallinn.ee): The official site provides detailed route maps, schedules, and real-time updates on bus locations.

- Mobile Apps: Apps like Google Maps and Citymapper offer real-time navigation and public transportation options, including bus routes and times.

Tourist Information Centers:
- Tourist information centers located throughout the city provide maps, schedules, and assistance for navigating the bus system.

Popular Bus Lines and Destinations

Old Town (Vanalinn):
- Bus Lines: Several lines, including 1A, 2, and 5, pass near or through the Old Town.
- Travel Time: From Viru Keskus, it takes approximately 5-10 minutes to reach the Old Town.

Kadriorg Palace:

- Bus Lines: Line 3 is a popular choice for reaching Kadriorg Palace and its surrounding park.

- Travel Time: From Viru Keskus, the journey takes about 10-15 minutes.

Pirita Beach:

- Bus Lines: Line 1A and 8 provide direct routes to Pirita Beach.

- Travel Time: From the city center, it takes around 20-25 minutes to reach the beach.

Tallinn TV Tower:

- Bus Lines: Line 34A and 38 connect the city center to the TV Tower.

- Travel Time: The trip from Viru Keskus takes approximately 30-35 minutes.

Telliskivi Creative City:

- Bus Lines: Lines 40 and 59 serve this trendy area.

- Travel Time: It's about a 15-20 minute ride from the city center.

Warnings and Tips for Travelers

Peak Hours:
- Morning and Evening Rush: Buses can be crowded during peak hours (7:30-9:00 AM and 4:30-6:30 PM). Plan your trips accordingly to avoid the busiest times.

Ticketing and Validation:
- Purchase and Validate Tickets: Tickets can be bought from kiosks, online, or through the mobile app. Remember to validate your ticket upon boarding to avoid fines.
- Free Public Transport: Residents with an ID card can travel for free on public transportation. Tourists must purchase tickets.

Safety and Security:

- Keep Belongings Safe: Be mindful of your belongings, especially in crowded buses. Pickpocketing, though not common, can occur.
- Avoid Night Travel Alone: While Tallinn is generally safe, it's advisable to avoid traveling alone late at night. Stick to well-lit areas and busier routes.

Accessibility:

- Wheelchair Accessible Buses: Most of Tallinn's buses are equipped with facilities for passengers with disabilities. Check the transport website for specific information.
- Priority Seating: Leave priority seats for those in need, such as elderly passengers, pregnant women, and those with disabilities.

Language Barriers:

- Language Assistance: While many drivers and passengers may speak English, it's helpful to know some basic Estonian phrases or have a translation app handy.

- Signage: Most bus signs and information are available in Estonian. Familiarize yourself with key terms or use apps to assist in translation.

Tallinn's bus system is a reliable and efficient way to explore the city. With a well-connected network of lines covering major attractions and residential areas, getting around is straightforward for both locals and tourists. By staying informed about routes, ticketing, and safety tips, you can ensure a smooth and enjoyable travel experience in Estonia's capital.

Conclusion

Tallinn, Estonia's capital, is a mesmerizing location that flawlessly blends rich history, vibrant culture, and modern charm. This book aims to provide detailed information for those who want to discover the city's magnificent surroundings and immerse themselves in its distinct ambiance.

Tallinn's Old Town, a UNESCO World Heritage site, serves as the city's center, taking visitors on a mesmerizing trip through medieval streets, historic sites, and a bustling cultural scene. From the landmark Toompea Castle to the beautiful Alexander Nevsky Cathedral, each corner of the Old Town tells a story about the city's past.

Beyond its ancient beauty, Tallinn embraces modernity through innovation and technological developments. The e-Estonia Showroom demonstrates the country's dedication to technological growth by highlighting the impact of e-governance and digital infrastructure on Estonian society.

Tallinn's diversified cultural landscape, emphasized by local festivals, events, and one-of-a-kind experiences, enables visitors to connect with the city more deeply. Whether it's tasting traditional Estonian cuisine, learning about maritime history at the Seaplane Harbour, or taking a Skywalk atop the Tallinn TV Tower, these activities make for a diverse and enjoyable vacation.

Tallinn's natural beauty goes beyond its historical core. From the gorgeous Pirita Beach to the peaceful Kakumäe Beach, the city provides a diverse coastline experience. Each beach has its own distinct charm, offering chances for leisure, water sports, and immersive nature experiences.

Accommodation options are diverse, ranging from boutique hotels in the Old Town to innovative stays such as the themed CRU Hotel. Travelers can select rooms that match their tastes, assuring a comfortable and enjoyable stay in Tallinn.

Tallinn has an efficient public transportation system and car rental choices. Navigating the city and its surroundings is simple, allowing visitors to experience both the ancient sites of Tallinn and the lovely landscapes of the surrounding areas.

The guide also provides practical advice for tourists on currency, language, safety, and local customs. Understanding these intricacies improves the whole travel experience, resulting in a smooth and comfortable stay in the Estonian capital.

Travelers who explore the top sites, hidden jewels, and cultural events described in this guide will go on a trip through Tallinn's soul. Whether they are charmed by the medieval architecture, mesmerized by the coastal vistas, or intrigued by the blend of tradition and innovation, visitors to Tallinn depart with an array of memories that connect the city's history, present, and future.

Tallinn, with its distinct blend of history, culture, and modernity, welcomes visitors to explore, discover, and connect with a city that honors its past while welcoming the possibilities of the future.

Printed in Great Britain
by Amazon